# teacher's friend publications

# SPRING!
## idea book

## a creative idea book
## for the
## elementary teacher

written and illustrated
by
## Karen Sevaly

poems by
Margaret Bolz

Copyright © 1990, 2001
Teacher's Friend, a Scholastic Company.
All rights reserved.
Printed in China.

ISBN-13 978-0-439-49962-0
ISBN-10 0-439-49962-3

# Table of Contents

**This book is dedicated to teachers and children everywhere!**

# Notes:

# Let's Make It!

# Let's Make It!

Children are especially responsive to the various holidays and themes associated with the four seasons. With this in mind, Teacher's Friend has published the "Spring" Idea Book to assist teachers in motivating students.

## WHO USES THIS BOOK:

Preschool and elementary teachers along with scout leaders, Sunday school teachers and parents all love the monthly and seasonal idea books. Each idea or craft can easily be adapted to fit a wide range of abilities and grade levels. Kindergartners can color and cut out the simple, bold patterns while older students love expanding these same patterns to a more complex format. Most of the ideas and activities are open-ended. Teachers may add their own curriculum appropriate for the grade level they teach. Young children may practice number, color or letter recognition while older students may like to drill multiplication facts or match homophones.

## WHAT YOU'LL FIND IN THIS BOOK:

Teachers and parents will find a variety of crafts, activities, bulletin board ideas and patterns that complement the monthly holidays and seasonal themes. Children will be delighted with the booklet cover, bingo cards, nametags, mobiles, place cards, writing pages and game boards. There is also a special section devoted to the sport of the season!

## HOW TO USE THIS BOOK:

Every page of this book may be

duplicated for individual classroom use. Some pages are meant to be used as duplicating masters or student worksheets. Most of the crafts and patterns may be copied onto construction paper or printed on index paper. Children can then make the crafts by coloring them using crayons or colored markers and cutting them out. Many of the pages can be enlarged with an overhead or opaque projector. The patterns can then be used for door displays, bulletin boards or murals.

Making mobiles is especially fun for all ages. Teachers may like to simplify mobile construction for young children by using one of these ideas.

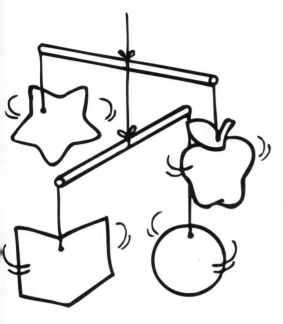

### DRINKING STRAW MOBILE

Thread a piece of yarn through a plastic drinking straw and tie a mobile pattern to each end. Flatten a paper clip and bend it around the center of the straw for hanging. The mobile can easily be balanced by adjusting the yarn. (Older students can make their mobiles the same way but may wish to add additional levels by hanging other mobiles directly below the first.)

### CLOTHES HANGER MOBILE

Mobiles can easily be made with a wire clothes hanger, as shown. Just tie each pattern piece to the hanger with thread, yarn or kite string.

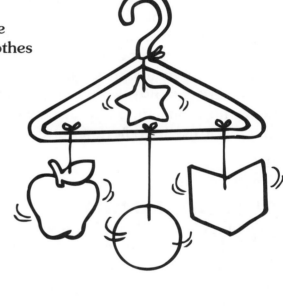

### YARN MOBILE

Gluing the pattern pieces to a length of yarn makes the most simple mobile, each piece spaced directly beneath the other. Tie a bow at the top and hang in a window or from the ceiling.

### CLIP ART PAGES:

The illustrations on these pages may be used in classroom bulletins, newsletters, notes home or just to decorate your own worksheets. Copy the clip art pages, cut out the illustrations you want, and paste them to your original before printing. The drawings may be enlarged or reduced on a copy machine. You are also free to enlarge the illustrations for other uses, such as bulletin boards, calendar decorations, booklet covers and awards.

### PLACE CARDS OR NAMETAGS:

If possible, laminate the finished nametags or place cards after you have copied them onto colored index paper. Use a dry transfer marker or dark crayon to write each name on the laminated surface. After the special day, simply wipe off the names with a tissue for use at another time.

## POETRY:

Children love simple, clever poetry. Use the poems in this book to inspire your students. You may want to have the students rewrite the poems for a timely record of their advancing handwriting skills.

Each morning, copy one or two lines, or an entire poem, on the class board. Ask the children to copy it in their best handwriting. Instruct them to write the date at the top of the page. Collect the poem pages and organize them chronologically in individual folders. This is a great way to show parents how their child's handwriting has improved throughout the year.

## STAND-UP CHARACTERS:

All of the stand-up characters in this book can easily be made from construction or index paper. Children can add the color and cut them out. The characters can be used as table decorations, name cards or used in a puppet show. Several characters can also be joined at the hands, as shown. The characters can also be enlarged on poster board for a bulletin board display or reduced in size for use in a diorama or as finger puppets.

## BULLETIN BOARDS:

Creating clever bulletin boards can be a fun experience for you and your students. Many of the bulletin board ideas in this book contain patterns that the students can make themselves. You simply need to cover the board with bright paper and display the appropriate heading. Students can make their own shamrocks for a classroom, flower garden or creative writing kites for a weather display.

Many of the illustrations in this book can also be enlarged and displayed on a bulletin board. Use an overhead or opaque projector to do your enlargements. When you enlarge a character, think BIG! Figures three, four or even five feet tall can make a dramatic display. Use colored butcher paper for large displays eliminating the need to add color with markers or crayons.

## WHATEVER YOU DO...

Have fun using the ideas in this book. Be creative! Develop your own ideas and adapt the patterns and crafts to fit your own curriculum. By using your imagination, you will be encouraging your students to be more creative. A creative classroom is a fun classroom! One that promotes an enthusiasm for learning!

# SPRING

*SPRINGTIME ACTIVITIES*

*SPRINGTIME SEQUENCE CARDS*

*SPRING BULLETIN BOARDS*

*DANCING FLOWERS*

*SPRINGTIME MOBILE*

*LADYBUG AND FLOWER MATCH*

*FLOWER POWER WRITING PAGE*

# SPRINGTIME ACTIVITIES!

## SPRINGTIME RAIN

Grab your umbrella, hold tight and stay under.
A cloudburst brings rain and lightning and thunder.
An umbrella in spring, you should never forget.
For one thing is certain, rain always is wet.

## SPRINGTIME GARDENS

As part of your science program, ask students to plant a variety of springtime gardens!

## AQUARIUM TERRARIUMS

One suggestion might be to have students use an old aquarium, turning it into plant terrarium. Use a planting mix purchased from a local nursery and ask students to plant seeds or small plants. They may like to keep records of the daily care and the growth of each plant.

## EGG CARTON GARDENS

Many different types of seeds can successfully be sprouted in Styrofoam egg cartons. Make sure that you punch a small hole in the bottom of each compartment for drainage. Fill the compartments with planting mix and let students plant the seeds. Place the cartons in a sunny window and have your students observe which type of seeds grow most quickly. (Water sparingly.)

## GROWING SPROUTS

Have students sprout avocado seeds or sweet potatoes in water. Alfalfa seeds are also easy to grow in the classroom and can later be eaten in student-made sandwiches.

# SPRING BINGO!

This game offers a fun way to introduce students to the spring season. Give each child a copy of the bingo words listed below or write the words on the chalkboard. Ask students to write any 24 words on his or her bingo card. Use the same directions you might use for regular bingo.

| | | | |
|---|---|---|---|
| SPRING | WEATHER | GREEN | ARBOR DAY |
| MARCH | WINDY | PASSOVER | TREES |
| APRIL | KITE | EASTER | MOTHER'S DAY |
| MAY | RAINY | EGGS | GIFTS |
| FLOWERS | UMBRELLA | HATCH | MAY DAY |
| COLORFUL | RAINBOW | BASKET | MEMORIAL DAY |
| BLOOM | SUNSHINE | BUNNY | BUTTERFLIES |
| BUD | SAINT PATRICK | GRASS | BUGS |
| LEAVES | SHAMROCK | APRIL FOOL'S | BEES |
| GROW | LEPRECHAUN | JOKES | INSECTS |

# SPRING NEWS!
## A NOTE HOME TO PARENTS!

_____

_____

_____

_____

_____

_____

_____

_____

_____

_____

_____

_____

_____

_____

_____

_____

_____

_____

_____

_____

_____

_____

# SPRINGTIME SEQUENCE CARDS!

# SPRING BULLETIN BOARDS!

## SOARING HIGH!

Display a large paper kite on the class bulletin board to encourage and motivate your students in specific areas.  As each student accomplishes a required task, reward him or her with his or her own kite bow.  Children will love seeing their names prominently displayed.

This easy idea can also be used to introduce new vocabulary words, mathematical concepts or as a way to welcome students to class that first day!

## POINT OUT THE BEST!

Emphasize the importance of weekly or daily lessons by "pointing" it out to your students!  By using the pattern on the next page, you can "point" out important calendar events, classroom monitors, or the letter or color of the week. Children can assist you in changing the board.

## TIME TO BLOOM!

Most classroom clocks have a round face, perfect for the center of a large paper flower!  Cut a circle the size of your clock face in the center of a piece of poster board. Cut large paper petals and leaves from colored construction paper and staple them around the hole.  Glue bits of fluffy tissue paper to the edge of the circle and place the entire flower over the face of your clock.  What an easy, colorful way to celebrate the blooming of spring!

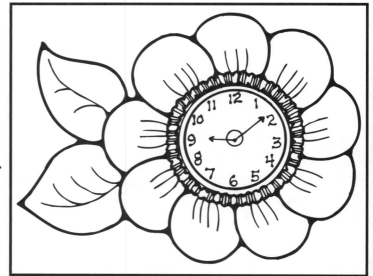

# Hand Pattern!

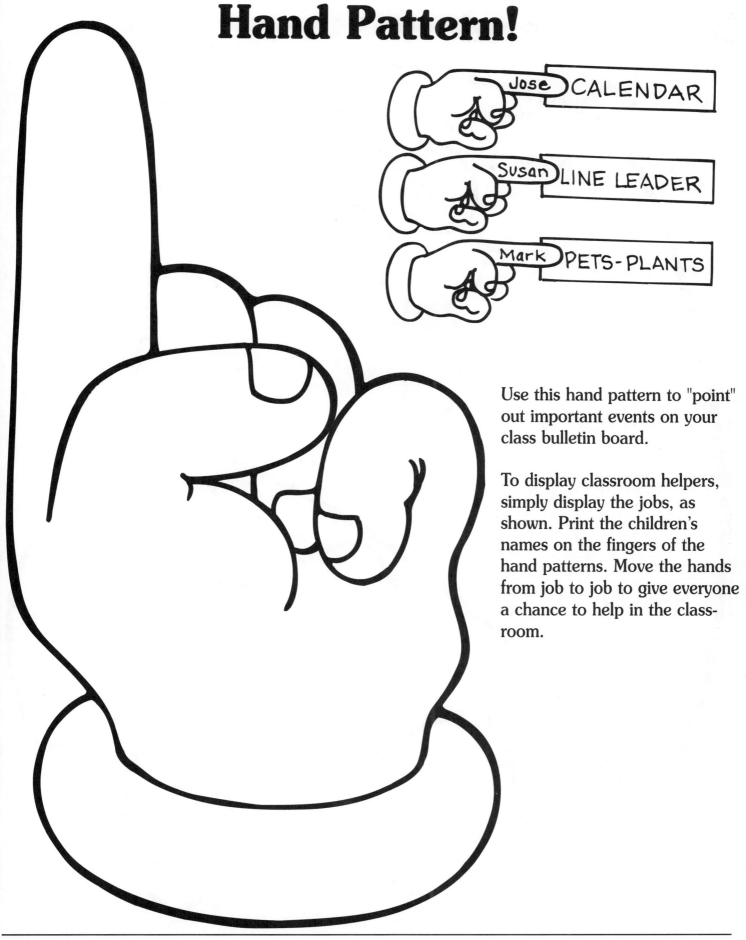

Jose CALENDAR

Susan LINE LEADER

Mark PETS-PLANTS

Use this hand pattern to "point" out important events on your class bulletin board.

To display classroom helpers, simply display the jobs, as shown. Print the children's names on the fingers of the hand patterns. Move the hands from job to job to give everyone a chance to help in the classroom.

# Kite Pattern!

18    TF1603 Spring Idea Book

# Dancing Flowers!

Cut the "Dancing Flowers" from colored paper. Color with markers or crayons. Use brass fasteners to assemble at the dots.

Children will enjoy making the "Dancing Flowers" and displaying them on the class bulletin board.

You might want to caption the board, "Boogie With The Best!" Have students write their own names down the stems.

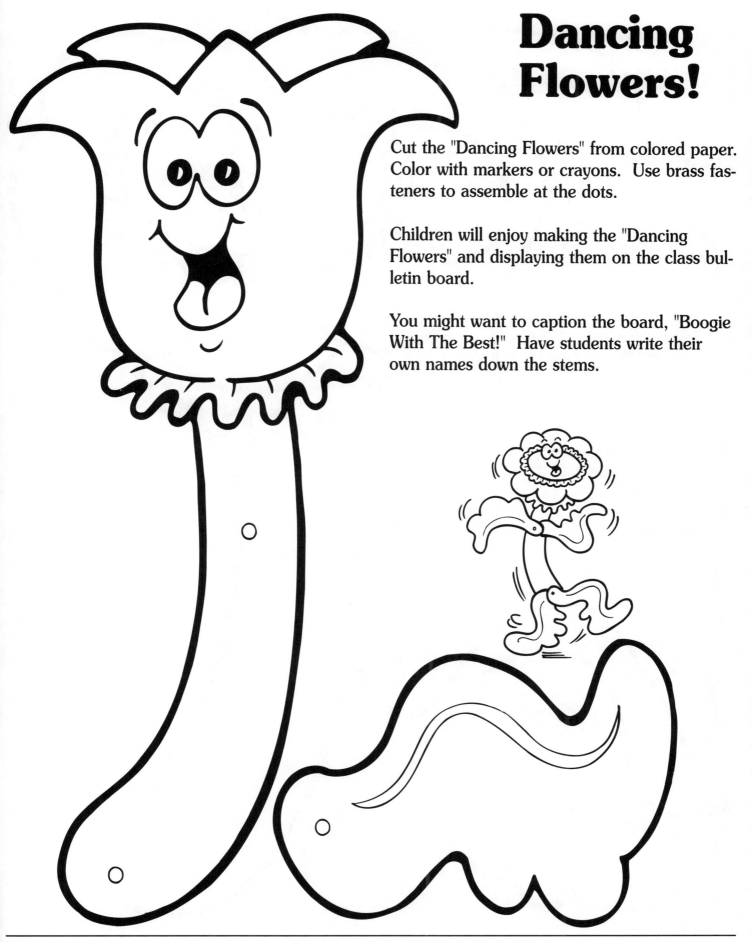

# Springtime Mobile!

Each student can make his or her own "Springtime Mobile" using these simple patterns.

Cut the patterns from index or construction paper and assemble with thread or yarn, as shown.

# Umbrella Pattern!

Cut this umbrella pattern from construction paper. Fold along the dotted lines and tape together. Thread a piece of yarn through the top of the handle and then through the umbrella top and hang.

# Stained Glass Butterflies!

These "Stained Glass Butterflies" are strikingly beautiful and simple to make.

You will need the following materials:

Several permanent colored markers          Black construction paper
Plastic food-storage wrap          Cellophane tape
Aluminum foil          8" paper plate

**Step One** - Tape one of the butterfly patterns to a smooth desktop. Ask each child to stretch a piece of plastic wrap over the pattern and tape in place. Instruct the children to color the plastic-covered butterflies using the colored markers. When the children finish coloring, have them trace the black lines using a black permanent marker.

**Step Two** - Have the students take a one-foot square of foil and crumple it carefully. Have each student open the foil and then gently spread it over a paper plate, taping it in place.

**Step Three** – Instruct each student to now remove his or her colored butterfly picture from the desktop and place it over the foil. Mount the finished projects on pieces of black construction paper and hang them in a window or display them on the class board.

# Ladybug and Flower Match!

15-8=

7

Making several ladybugs and flowers from colored construction paper can easily make several matching activities.

For a math activity, label each flower with a problem and each ladybug with an appropriate answer. Long and short vowel sounds can easily be practiced with the same type of matching activity. Label each flower with a short or long vowel. Write words appropriate to the sounds on the flowers and have students match them to the correct ladybug.

FLOWER POWER!

# SUPER STUDENT AWARD!

awarded to

_____

for

_____

_____

_____

_____

Date

_____

Teacher

## March

## STUDENT OF THE MONTH

### AWARDED TO

_____

Name

_____

_____  _____
Teacher              Date

# MARCH NEWSLETTER!

| TEACHER: | RM# | DATE: |
|---|---|---|

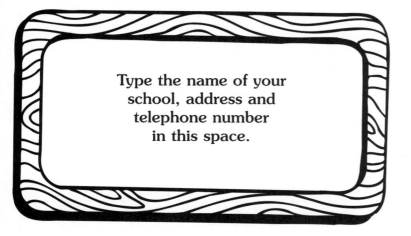

Type the name of your
school, address and
telephone number
in this space.

## SUGGESTIONS FOR A MARCH NEWSLETTER:

- List the name of each student that was selected student of the week for the month of February.

- Note the days of the month, such as St. Patrick's Day. (Make sure that parents know which days children will not be in attendance if spring vacation falls within this month).

- Announce special programs or activities being conducted by your school or in your classroom.

- Tell about something special your class is currently working on.

- Ask your school principal to write a brief message that can be included with the March newsletter.

- Ask for parent volunteers or donations for the class St. Patrick's Day party. (Easter may also fall during the month of March.)

- Staple the March cafeteria menu to each newsletter.

- Send a welcome note to a new student or a get-well message to a student that has been out ill.

- Announce upcoming field trips, class plays or fund raisers.

# March Clip Art!

# MARCH BULLETIN BOARDS!

## HATS OFF!
Portray the winds of March by displaying flying hats across the class bulletin board. Children can bring hats from home to display or have them make the hats from the patterns found in this book. Add feathers, buttons, fabric and other novelties for decorations.

## GENTLE AS LAMBS!
What a great way to emphasize positive character traits to your students! Display a large lamb on the class board. Add cotton balls for his fluffy wool. With the help of your students, list the various qualities that make each of us a good friend and responsible citizen.

## GREAT WORK!
Emphasize the greatness of good classroom work by displaying this roaring lion! Children might like to write papers about things they find "Grrrrreat!"

# Roaring Lion!

**Gentle Lamb!**

36

# Hat Booklet!

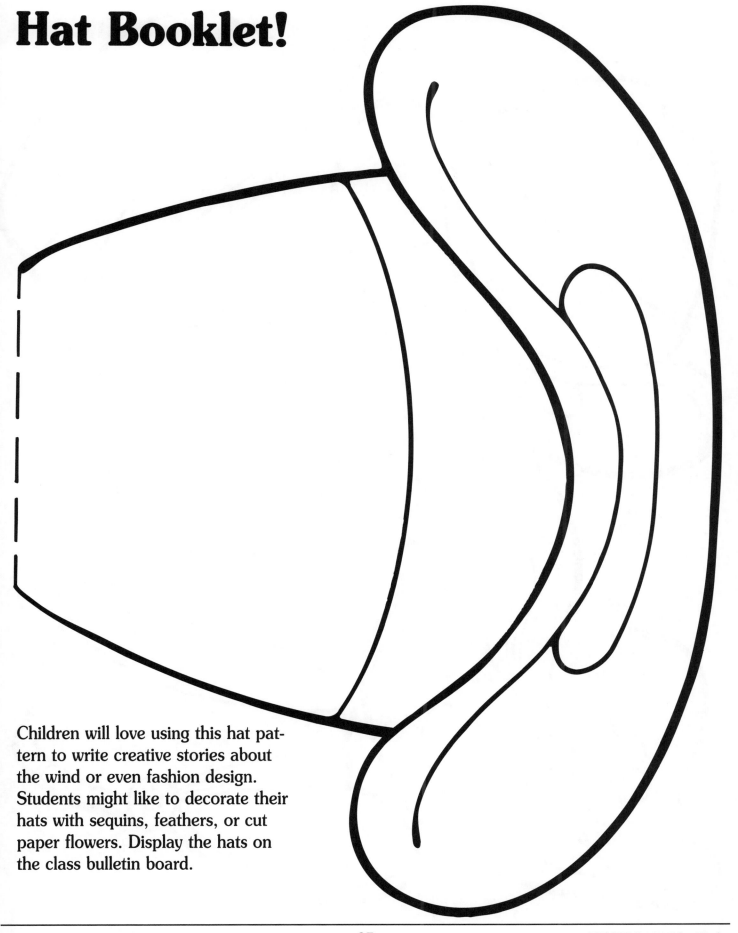

Children will love using this hat pattern to write creative stories about the wind or even fashion design. Students might like to decorate their hats with sequins, feathers, or cut paper flowers. Display the hats on the class bulletin board.

# MARCH ACTIVITIES!

## GREEN! GREEN!

Celebrate Saint Patrick's Day by providing a tasty treat for your students!

Green bell peppers offer an excellent source of vitamins and minerals. Along with generous amounts of ranch dressing, your students will gobble them up!

Bell peppers also provide an excellent way to stamp attractive shamrock designs. Cut the pepper in half, sideways, and clean out any seeds. Using green poster paint, dip the pepper in the paint and stamp it onto white paper.

A fun way to introduce a new vegetable to young children!

## MARCH BEGINNINGS!

March is when the earth's renewed,
A very pleasant interlude.
A new beginning bursts all over.
Everything turns green as clover.
March wind replaced by gentle breeze,
Flowers bloom and so do trees.
March is like a great invention,
But springtime sports get my attention!

## WINDY ACTIVITIES!

When March winds blow, ask your students to try some of these fun suggestions:

- Make paper airplanes and see which one flies the farthest.
- Have a balloon launch with messages inside.
- Make kites from paper lunch sacks and fly them during recess.
- Make Frisbees ® from disposable plastic plates. Children can decorate them with permanent colored markers.
- Make your own bubble wands from plastic six-pack holders. See who can get the most bubbles in the air at one time. (Make a bubble solution by mixing 1/2 cup liquid detergent, 1 quart water and a couple of tablespoons of white Karo ® syrup. Refrigerate overnight before using.)

# March Fun Glasses!

Cut Out

Cut Out

Cut the pattern pieces from heavy index paper and color with markers or crayons.

Attach the bows to the frame by fitting them into the designated slots.

# Stand-Up Shamrocks!

Cut out the pot of gold and shamrocks from heavy paper. Children can write their own springtime messages or names across the shamrocks. Fan-fold along the dotted lines. Glue the pot of gold to the first shamrock and stand it on a desktop for a March decoration.

TF1603 Spring Idea Book

# Leprechaun Character!

Cut this cute leprechaun from heavy index paper. Color him and fold along the dotted lines. Bend his arms forward and staple or paste the pot of gold to his hands.

Use the leprechaun as a table decoration for St. Patrick's Day!

TF1603 Spring Idea Book

# My
# Pot of Gold
# Story!

_____

# Mr. Shamrock!

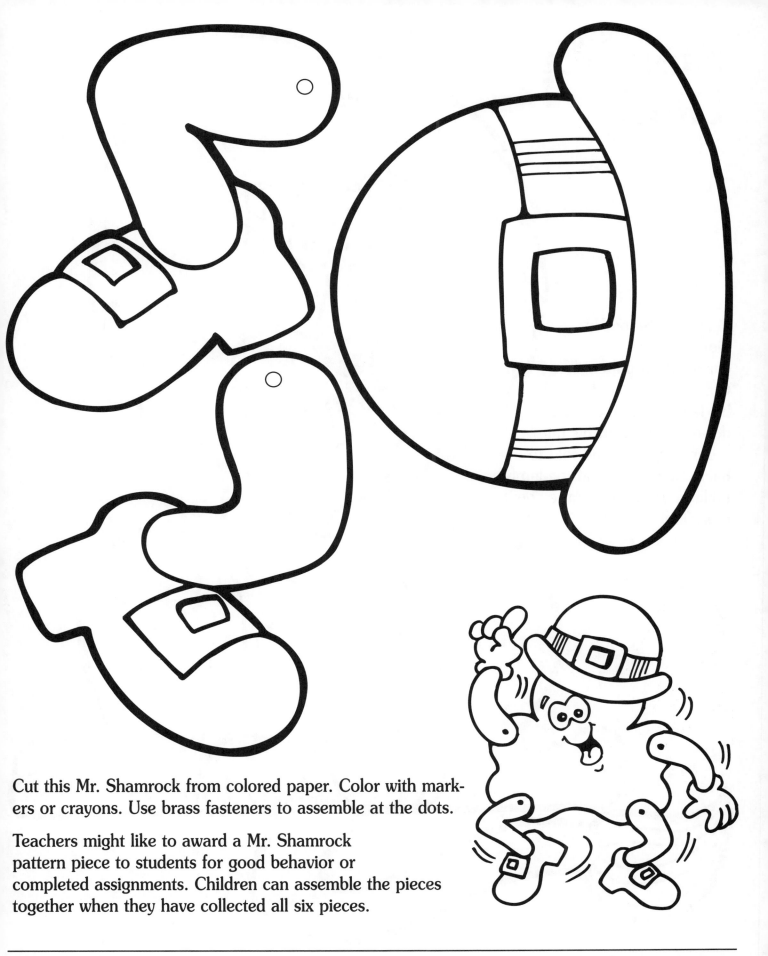

Cut this Mr. Shamrock from colored paper. Color with markers or crayons. Use brass fasteners to assemble at the dots.

Teachers might like to award a Mr. Shamrock pattern piece to students for good behavior or completed assignments. Children can assemble the pieces together when they have collected all six pieces.

# Stand-Up Lion!

Make this Stand-Up Lion from index or construction paper. Color, cut and fold. Fold his legs forward, along the dotted lines. Curl his tail around a pencil and fold to the back. Stand him and the lamb on a tabletop to celebrate the coming of spring!

# Stand-Up Lamb!

Make this Stand-Up Lamb from index or construction paper. Color, cut and fold.

You may want to glue white cotton balls to the lamb to simulate his fluffy wool.

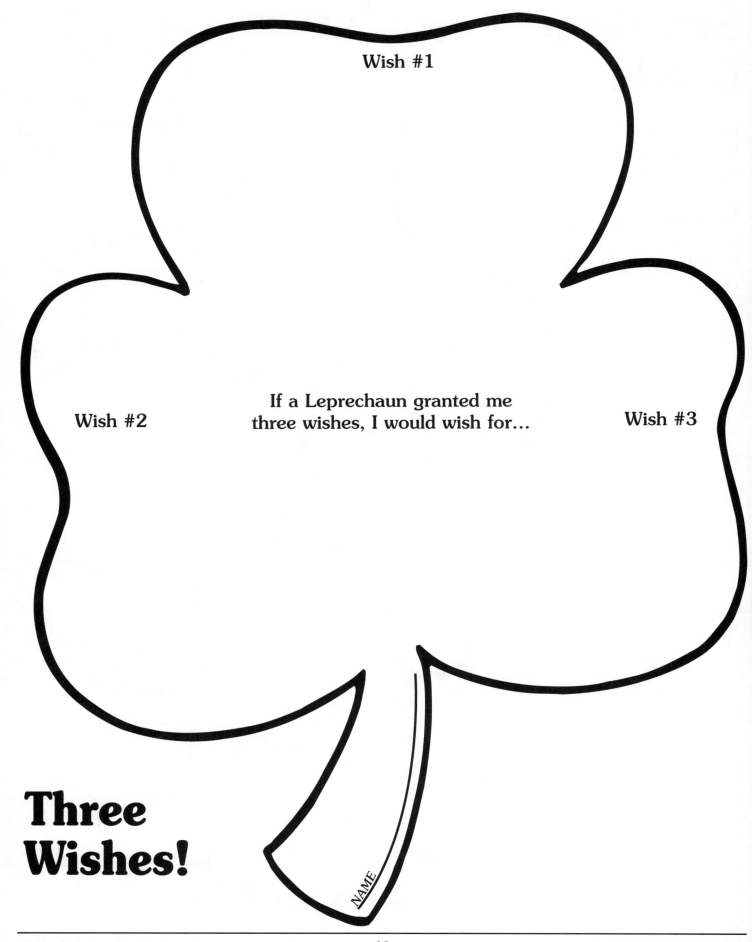

Wish #1

Wish #2

If a Leprechaun granted me
three wishes, I would wish for...

Wish #3

# Three Wishes!

NAME

# APRIL

APRIL AWARDS

APRIL CLIP ART

APRIL BULLETIN BOARDS

APRIL ACTIVITIES

APRIL FUN GLASSES

STAND-UP EASTER EGGS

STAND-UP BUNNY

BUNNY MASK AND EARS

APRIL SHOWERS MOBILE

APRIL FOOL'S DAY ACTIVITIES

ARBOR DAY ACTIVITIES

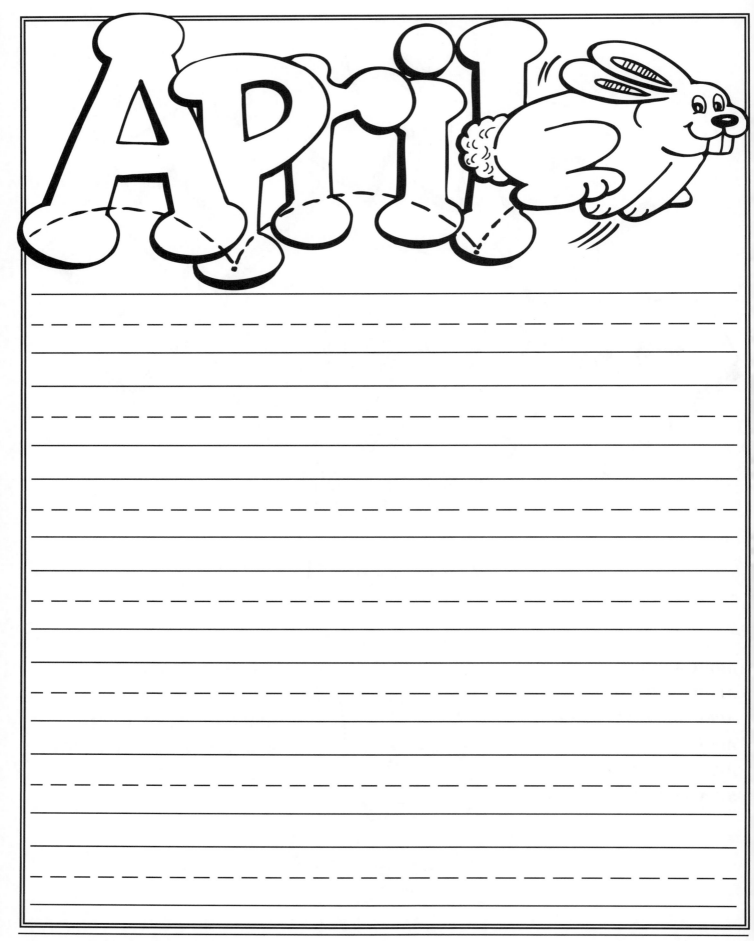

# SUPER STUDENT AWARD!

awarded to

_____

for

_____

_____

_____

_____

Date

_____

Teacher

---

# April

## STUDENT OF THE MONTH

### AWARDED TO

_____

Name

_____

_____        _____

Teacher                                    Date

---

                   TF1603 Spring Idea Book

# APRIL NEWSLETTER!

**TEACHER:**             **RM#**      **DATE:**

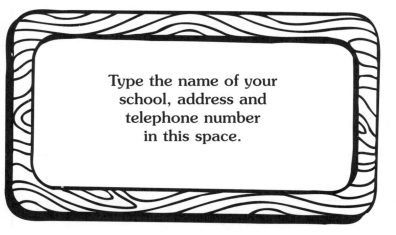

Type the name of your
school, address and
telephone number
in this space.

## SUGGESTIONS FOR AN APRIL NEWSLETTER:

- List the name of each student that was selected student of the week for the month of March.

- Note the dates of spring vacation and Easter. Make sure that parents know which days children will not be in attendance.

- Announce special activities or programs being conducted by your school or in your classroom.

- Tell about something special your class is currently working on.

- Ask one of your students to draw several small pictures about Easter to be used in the April newsletter.

- Ask your school principal to write a brief message that can be included with the April newsletter.

- Ask for parent volunteers or donations for the class Easter party or egg hunt.

- Staple the April cafeteria menu to each newsletter.

- Send a welcome note to a new student or a get-well message to a student that has been out ill.

- Include a joke or riddle in celebration of April Fool's Day.

# April Clip Art!

## LOOK WHAT'S HATCHING!

This goofy hatching chick will make your students giggle with delight!

Display him on the class bulletin board along with creative writing egg booklets made by your students. The egg booklets can be decorated with crayons or markers to resemble Easter eggs.

## SWINGING BUNNY!

Enlarge this cute bunny and display him on the class door or bulletin board. Glue on fluffy, white cotton balls for his tail and use real rope or cording for the swing ropes. A cute title might be, "Swing Into Spring!"

## COLOR YOUR WORLD...

Fluffy white clouds cut from polyester batting set off this colorful spring bulletin board. Various colors of twisted crepe paper strips form the rainbow. Children can write colorful poems that can be displayed around the board.

# Hatching Chick!

# Hatching Stories!

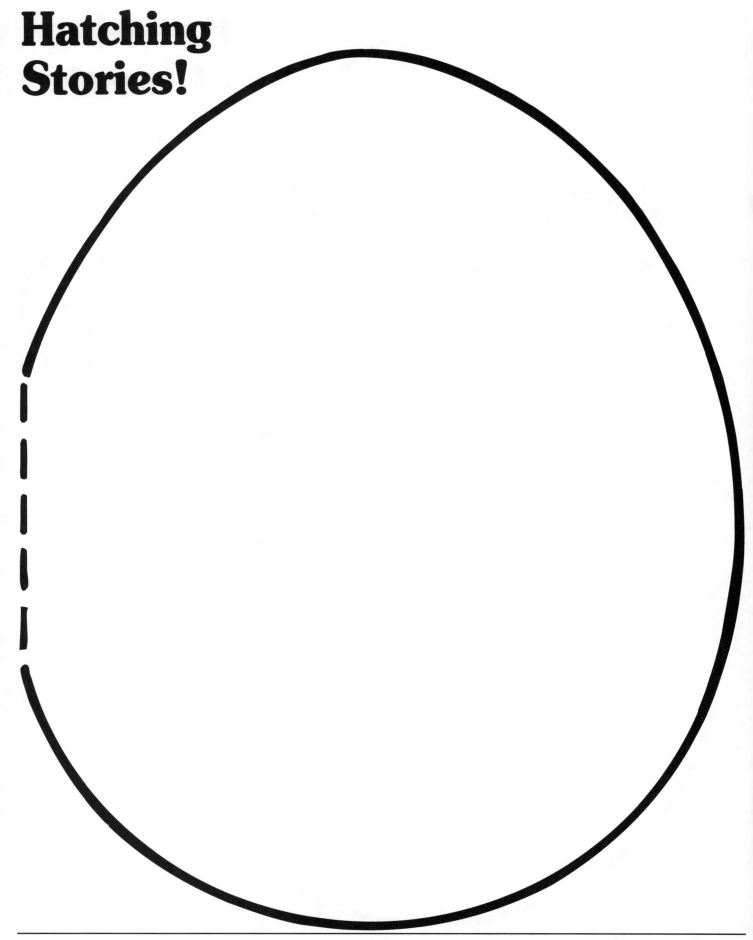

# Swinging Bunny!

# APRIL ACTIVITIES!

## APRIL

Depending on the tide and moon,
Easter may come late or soon.
In March or April, it changes around.
More often in April, it is found.

April Fool is the very first day.
On one another tricks we play.
April is beautiful with cool grass and flowers.
I wish it were longer by days and by hours.

Try these springtime activities:

## DAYLIGHT SAVINGS TIME!

It's time to spring forward with daylight savings time! Set your clocks one hour ahead of standard time and ask your students to observe the lengthening days. Students can chart the daylight hours by checking the daily newspaper for the time of each sunrise and sunset. Using a large graph, have them note these times. Draw lines from dot to dot to illustrate how the daylight hours are increasing.

## FREE TIME "EGGS"TRAVAGANZA

Bring a large Easter basket to school full of colorful plastic Easter eggs. As each student finishes his or her work, ask him or her to select an egg and do whatever is instructed on the slip of paper hidden inside. Some suggestions might be, "Make an Easter card for mom or dad," or "Be the first one excused at the next recess!"

The children will be eager to complete the day's work when such a fun Easter surprise awaits them!

## EASTER EGGS

My Easter basket has inside
Easter eggs that have been dyed,
Pretty eggs the chickens laid,
Decorated and displayed.

Boiled eggs in soft pastels
And pictures painted on the shells.
Like rainbow colors in the sky,
So are the colors in the dye.

Every year this great tradition
Leaves me with a firm decision,
Although egg dyeing is great fun,
Afterwards, to eat each one.

Eating Easter eggs I peel
Day after day, for many a meal.
This decision can't be truer,
"Maybe, next year, I'll dye fewer!"

---

# April Fun Glasses!

Cut the pattern pieces from heavy index paper and color with markers or crayons. Attach the bows to the frame by fitting them into the designated slots.

Children will love making and wearing these "April Fun Glasses" at Easter time!

Cut Out

Cut Out

# Stand-Up Easter Eggs!

Cut the Easter eggs and bunny from heavy paper. Write your own Easter messages across the eggs. Fanfold along the dotted lines. Glue the bunny to the first egg and stand it on a desktop for an Easter decoration.

MY BUNNY BOOK

TF1603 Spring Idea Book

# Stand-Up Bunny!

Make this cute bunny character from index paper.
Color, cut out and fold.
Bend his arms forward and
staple or paste the
basket to his hands.

# Bunny Mask and Ears!

Cut these cute bunny mask and ears patterns from colored construction paper. Glue the ears to the top of the mask, as shown. Students might like to add pipe cleaner whiskers to the mask. Tie the mask to the back of the head with heavy kite string.

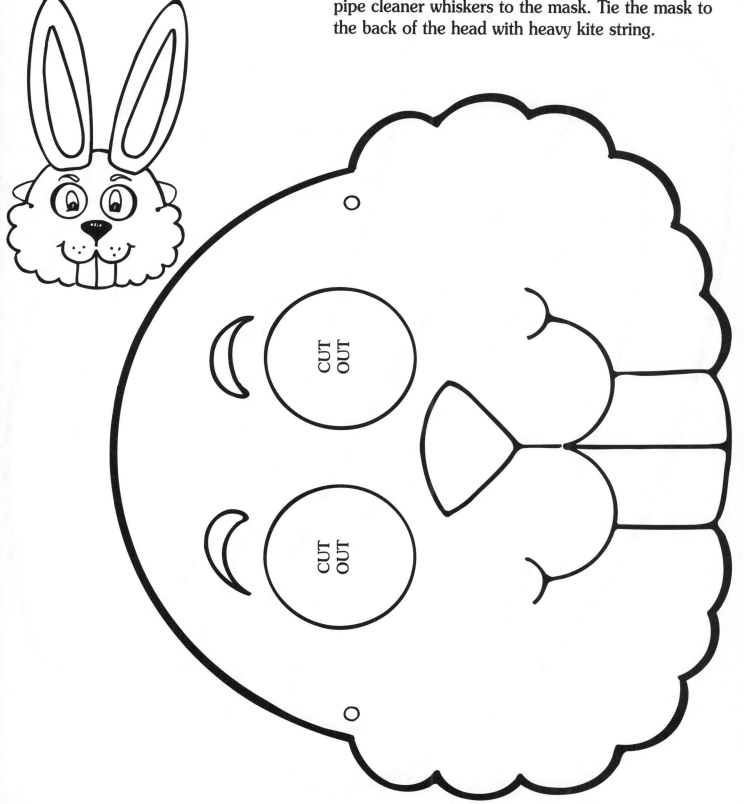

CUT OUT

CUT OUT

These bunny ears can also be attached to a paper headband and worn by children during the annual Easter egg hunt!

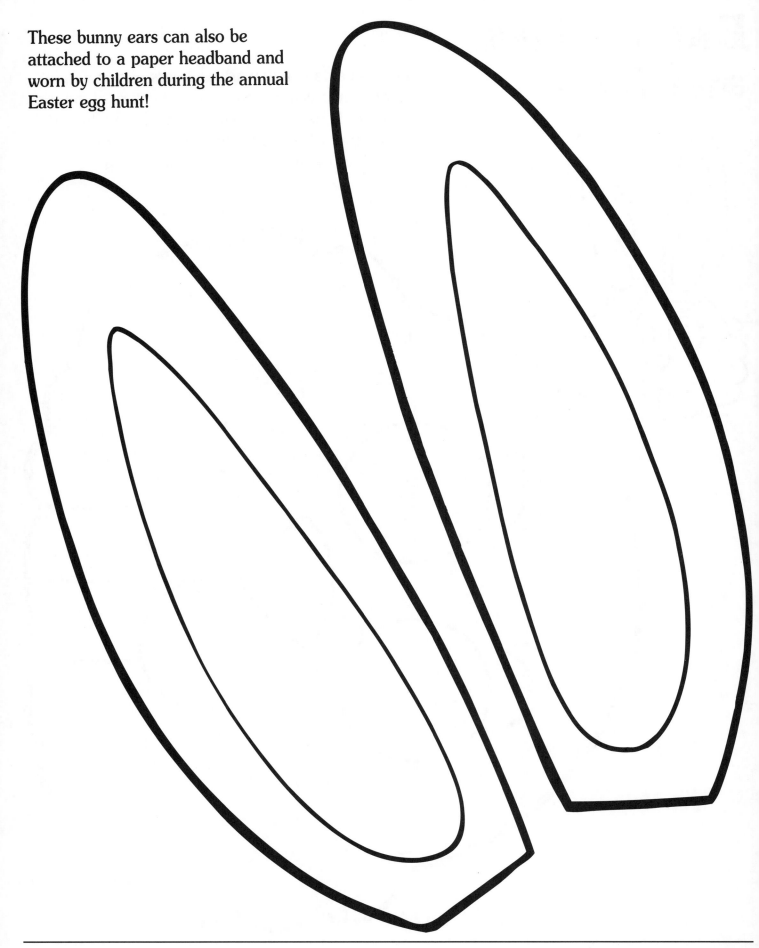

# Egg Holders!

Cut these egg holders from heavy index or construction paper. Color with crayons or markers. Write your own springtime or Easter message on either side of the characters. Glue or staple the two ends together to form a loop and stand a hard-boiled egg inside. This is a cute way to display your decorated eggs during this spring holiday!

These holders can also be used as Easter napkin rings for your holiday dinner table!

Your students might enjoy coloring Easter eggs in the classroom. Try some of these unusual ways of dyeing eggs:

Soak various colors of crepe paper in small cups of hot water. Dye the eggs the same way you would using a commercial egg dye.

A small flower or leaf can be placed on the eggshell and then wrapped tightly with a nylon stocking. After dyeing, remove the nylon and leaf to reveal a beautiful, natural design!

Wrap your eggs with rubber bands and then dye them. Remove the rubber bands to reveal the interesting designs.

Use vegetables to dye your eggs! Spinach or onion skins boiled on a stovetop work very well. You might also want to experiment with teabags or beets!

APRIL SHOWERS BRING MAY FLOWERS

NAME

# April Showers Bring May Flowers Mobile

Each child can make his or her own "April Showers Mobile" by cutting these pattern pieces from colored construction paper. (They may want to mount the finished pieces on poster board for added durability.)

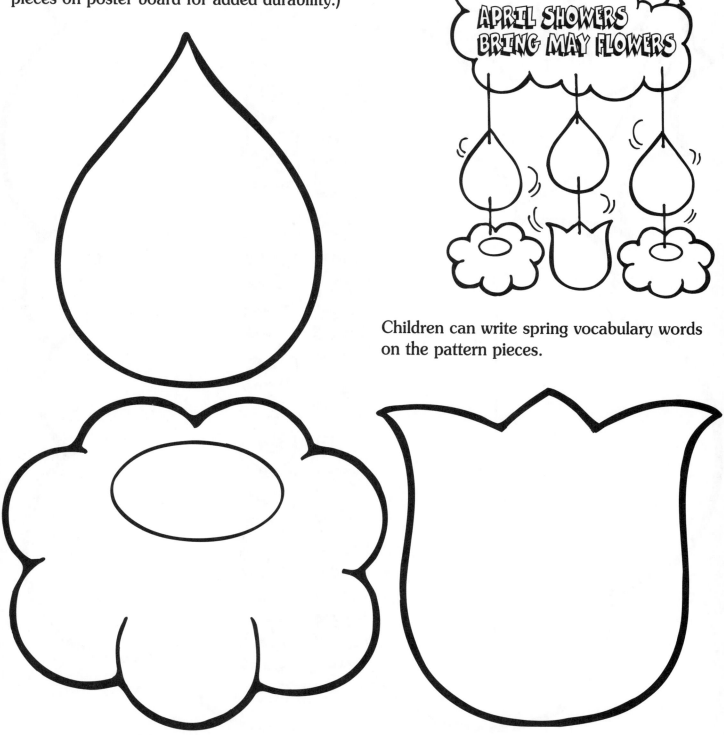

Children can write spring vocabulary words on the pattern pieces.

# APRIL FOOL'S DAY ACTIVITIES!

April is National Humor month, a perfect time to explore the funny world in which we live. (Remember, April 1st is April Fool's Day!)

Suggest some of these "funny" activities to your students:

## FUNNY PAPERS

Start a collection of comic strips on the class bulletin board. Ask children to gather cartoons and comic strips found in magazines and newspapers. They may also like to write and draw their own cartoons that can be featured on the board. Soon your bulletin board will be filled with a variety of illustrations, guaranteed to liven up any school day!

## COMEDY HOUR

Children will love being in the spotlight, acting out their own jokes and riddles.

Ask students to gather their favorite skits or jokes to act out. (They should write the jokes out before performing them in front of the class.) Encourage them to use props if they like.

Make a microphone from a paper tube and black yarn. Darken the room and put your class comedian in a spotlight (flashlight) when he or she performs. The class can act as an audience, applauding after each comedian has performed.

## APRIL FOOL'S ELF

Delight your students on the first of April by having an April Fool's Elf visit the classroom. When students arrive that morning, they each find a part of a secret message taped to the top of his or her desk. (Write the entire message on a large sheet of butcher paper. Cut the message into sections, numbering each one for easier deciphering.) Have the students arrange the message in order and read the entire message out loud. This message can tell cute things about themselves. Or, have the elf ask them to do particular activities during the day, such as drawing pictures of the elf, writing letters or cleaning out their desks. Later in the day, another message can be left, directing them to a special ice cream treat!

You might want to extend the elf's visit for several days. His presence can be used to motivate children with better behavior or improved study skills. Make sure to take care that the students never suspect that you are the April Fool's Elf!

This fun activity can also be used on March 17th, Saint Patrick's Day. Simply change the elf to a leprechaun!

# My Favorite April Fool's Joke

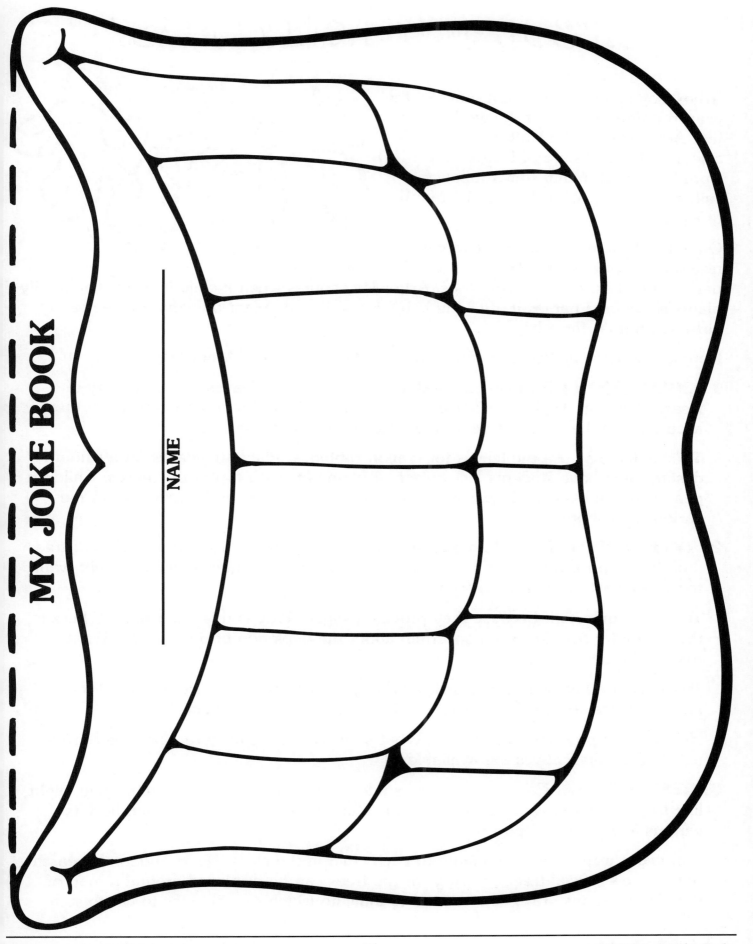

MY JOKE BOOK

NAME

# ARBOR DAY ACTIVITIES!

Arbor Day comes at different times of the year in different parts of the world. The first Arbor Day in the United States was celebrated in the state of Nebraska on April 22, 1872. Many states followed suit, celebrating Arbor Day in the month of April.

On Arbor Day, many schools and civic organizations plant one or more trees to beautify their parks and cities. In some countries, Arbor Day comes when a child is born. The family plants a tree and names it after the baby. Some people plant one kind of tree for a girl and another for a boy.

Here are some activities that can be used to help recognize Arbor Day:

1. **COLLECTION OF LEAVES** – Ask children to collect leaves from a variety of trees. They can display the leaves on the class bulletin board and categorize them according to the type of tree such as deciduous, evergreen, etc.

   They could also use the leaves for crayon rubbings. Place the leaves on a smooth desktop and have students lay a piece of plain paper on top of the leaves. Children gently crayon over the leaves creating interesting designs and textures from the various leaf shapes.

2. **TREE QUESTIONS** – Hold a class discussion regarding the various types of trees and the purpose they serve in our world. Here are a few questions you might want to use to start off your discussion.

   Trees are important because they provide oxygen. Why is this important? Where in the world are people most concerned about the depletion of our forests? What reason do they give?

   Trees are used in various industries. What products are made from trees? What types of trees are used? What types of jobs rely on tree products?

   How can we preserve our forests? What steps can we take to recycle wood products? What alternatives are available?

3. **RESEARCH TREES** – Assign each student a type of tree to research. They might like to include a drawing of their tree, explain its seasonal changes and lists its various functions and purposes.

   You might want to assign a state to each child in the class. Have students research their state's official tree. Drawings of the trees can be displayed around a map of the United States. Yarn can be used to indicate which tree belongs to which state.

---

# My Tree

Name of my tree:

_____

My tree is...

Evergreen ☐     Hardwood ☐

Deciduous ☐     Softwood ☐

Where my tree grows: _____

_____

_____

_____

Products made from my tree:

My tree drawing

bark drawing     leaf drawing

_____     _____

_____     _____

_____     _____

Some interesting things about my tree: _____

_____

_____

What I like best about my tree: _____

_____

# My Tree Report

MAY AWARDS

STAND-UP FLOWERS

MAY CLIP ART

MOTHER'S DAY ACTIVITIES

MAY ACTIVITIES

STAND-UP MOM

MAY BULLETIN BOARDS

MAKE MOM HAPPY GAME

MAY FUN GLASSES

MOTHER'S DAY COUPON BOOK

TF1603 Spring Idea Book

# SUPER STUDENT AWARD!

awarded to

_____

for

_____

_____

_____

_____

Date

_____

Teacher

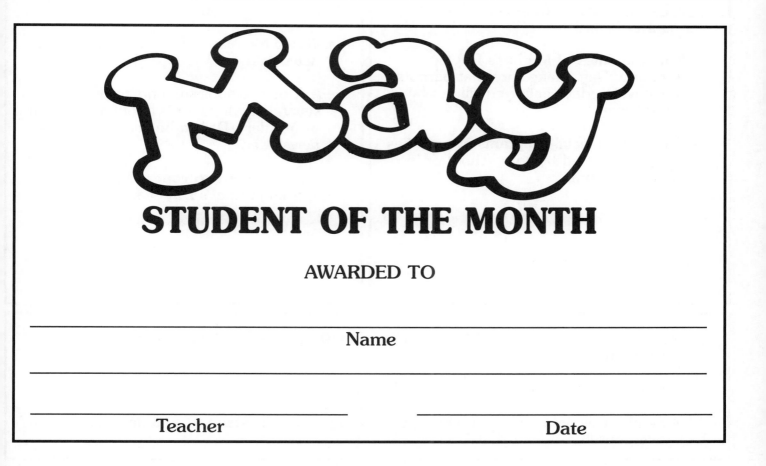

# May

## STUDENT OF THE MONTH

### AWARDED TO

_____

Name

_____

_____        _____
Teacher                              Date

# MAY NEWSLETTER!

**TEACHER:**               **RM#**      **DATE:**

Type the name of your school, address and telephone number in this space.

## SUGGESTIONS FOR A MAY NEWSLETTER:

- List the name of each student that was selected student of the week for the month of April.

- Note the dates of Mother's Day and Memorial Day. Make sure that parents know which days children will not be in attendance.

- Announce special programs or activities being conducted by your school or in your classroom.

- Tell about something special your class is currently working on.

- Staple the May cafeteria menu to each newsletter.

- Ask one of your students to draw several small pictures about springtime or Mother's Day to be used in the May newsletter.

- Invite mothers to your classroom for a special Mother's Day tea.

- Ask your school principal to write a brief message that can be included with the May newsletter.

- Announce upcoming field trips, fund raisers or testing dates.

- Send a welcome note to a new student or a get-well message to a student that has been out ill.

# May Clip Art!

# MAY ACTIVITIES!

## MAY

The end of May often has good weather,
a good time for families and friends to get together.
Picnic with a lunch mother made,
or sit on a curb to watch a parade.

Go to the beach for a swim and some fun,
or watch a ball game or play in one.
Memorial Day, near the end of spring,
use as you choose, any way, anything.

Some people choose this day
to honor those who've passed away.
This day is for the entire nation.
No school. No work. A day of vacation.

## CLASS FLOWER AND PLANT SHOW

A fun way to stimulate your students' interest and appreciation of May flowers is to arrange for a class flower and plant show.

Familiarize your students with common garden plants by using encyclopedias, seed catalogs and gardening books. You might like to ask a local gardener or horticulturist to visit your class and talk about his or her hobby or profession. Children grow their flowers and plants at home, and bring them to class on a special day.

Divide the show into several categories. Categories might include plants grown from seeds, fruits and vegetables, potted plants or flower arrangements. Ask students to draw posters and invitations announcing the show and post them around the school. (You might want to plan a date close to Mother's Day and encourage all mothers to come share in the experience.) On the day of the show, children vote for their favorite entry. Winners receive a special certificate or ribbon.

## CINCO DE MAYO – MAY 5TH

Cinco De Mayo is a wonderful time to teach students a little about Mexico.

As part of your celebration, make a colorful piñata with your students. Place two or three large grocery bags inside one another and fill with special treats. The children can add the decorations. Hang the piñata with a heavy cord and have the students take turns breaking it with a broomstick.

## CINCO DE MAYO

Dancing feet and clapping hands,
dance to Mariachi bands.
Violins play, trumpets blow,
festive day of Mexico.
Cinco De Mayo, day of fun.
Food and drink for everyone.
Next year, I'll come back for more,
Señorita and Señor!

---

# MAY BULLETIN BOARDS!

## FLY AWAY

These cute birds will fly across the class bulletin board to reach their goal of the birdhouse. Give each child a bird cut from colored paper. As books are read, or assignments completed, the birds fly toward their goal. Each bird, or child, who reaches the birdhouse should be awarded with a special treat.

## MERRY MAY MURAL

Cover a large bulletin board with blue butcher paper and divide your class into at least five groups. Give each group one phase of the mural to complete. Sky and clouds, trees, flowers, butterflies and birds, plus the title, are a few suggestions.

## GROW WITH US!

Display a large potted plant made from construction paper on the classroom door or bulletin board. Children draw self-portraits on small paper plates that are decorated as flowers. Arrange the flowers on the plant as a happy way to welcome everyone to your classroom!

# Blooming Flowers!

## LOOK WHO'S BLOOMING NOW!

Students will love creating their own flower garden on the class bulletin board.

Have each student cut a long stem and two leaves from green construction paper. Ask each child to write his or her name on the stem. Display these on the board with a catchy title.

As each child completes a required assignment, add a paper flower to the top of the stem. Glue a muffin paper to the inside of the flower for a three dimensional effect.

# Matching Birds and Birdhouses!

Make several copies of birds and birdhouses from colored construction paper. Use them in a variety of matching activities such as letter recognition, math facts, words and definitions, opposites and so on.

# Bird Mobile!

Cut these attractive bird patterns from heavy index paper and color each one with the appropriate colors.

Fold each bird at the center dotted line and fold each wing out. Punch holes where indicated and hang with a thread or fishing line.

Each child can make his or her own Bird Mobile by hanging all three birds from a tree twig, as shown.

**EASTERN BLUEBIRD**

TF1603 Spring Idea Book

**CARDINAL**

TF1603 Spring Idea Book

**ROBIN**

TF1603 Spring Idea Book

# May Fun Glasses!

Cut the pattern pieces from heavy index paper and color with markers or crayons. Attach the bows to the frame by fitting them into the designated slots.

# Stand-Up Flowers!

Cut out this cute character and flowers from heavy paper. Write your own message across the flowers. Fanfold along the dotted lines. Glue the character to the first flower and stand on a desk or use as a Mother's Day card.

# MOTHER'S DAY ACTIVITIES!

## A CHILD'S VIEW OF MOTHER'S DAY

When I am big, and old, and grown,
I will have children of my own.
I'll have a great big rocking chair,
And rock them while I'm sitting there.

I'll teach them colors, numbers, too,
And teach them how to tie a shoe.
When they are sick, I'll make them better.
When it is cold, they'll wear a sweater.

I'll wash their socks and underwear,
And all their meals I will prepare.
And if I have a girl or boy,
I'll play the games that they enjoy.

I will buy them what they need,
And I will teach them how to read.
I will teach them how to write,
And I'll be sure they sleep at night.

I'll teach them how to catch a ball,
And kiss their hurts if they should fall.
For every child, I'll work quite hard.
For me they'll make a Mother's Day card.

I think I'd better do that right now.
It's for my Mom. I should know how.
I'll write a card, "This is for you,
To thank you, Mom, for all you do."

"I'm glad that now when you are grown,
I have you, Mom, my very own!"

## THANK YOU, MOM

Ask children to think of ways in which they usually forget to thank their mothers. Have them write their special thank you notes on pastel colored paper and include it in a Mother's Day card!

## BABY NAMES

Most animals have specific names for the babies. See if your students can determine what types of animals have these babies:

| | |
|---|---|
| foal | pup |
| cub | kitten |
| calf | chick |
| duckling | piglet |
| whelp | lamb |
| gosling | bunny |
| joey | kid |
| fawn | |

## RECIPE FOR MOM

Children will love creating "MOM" recipes! Ask each child to write a recipe using the ingredients that make his or her mom special. Here is an example:

In a large bowl, combine 3 cups of happiness and 2 pounds of love. Gently stir together with a tablespoon of kindness, a dash of discipline and a sprinkle of patience. Slowly warm in a loving atmosphere and soon you'll have something special, my MOM!

# Woven Hearts!

This woven heart can be given to Mom for a simple Mother's Day gift. Fill it with small candies, notes of appreciation or wild flowers.

Cut two patterns from pastel colored construction paper. Fold each pattern in half and make three cuts down the center. Hold one piece in each hand and carefully weave the first piece in one hand over and under the piece in the other hand. Continue weaving each piece the same way. Attach a small paper handle to the top. When you are finished, your woven heart will look like the one above.

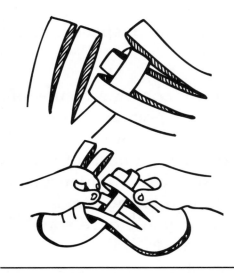

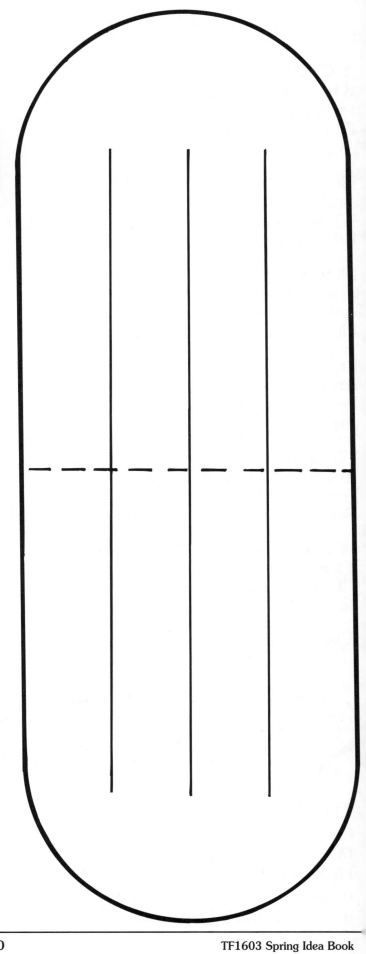

# Stand-Up Mom!

Make this Stand-Up Mom from index paper. Color, cut out and fold. Attach the heart to one hand and write a special message on her apron.

Stand her on a table for a Mother's Day decoration or give her as a card to your own mom on her special day!

# MAKE MOM

Two, three or four children can play this game. Each player rolls a die and moves the required spaces.

# HAPPY GAME

The player takes a task card and does what it says. The first player to reach the finish line is the winner. Children will love discovering ways to make Mom happy!

MESSY ROOM!
LOSE A TURN

FORGOT TO SET
THE TABLE!
GO BACK TWO
SPACES

LATE FOR DINNER!
GO BACK ONE SPACE

DID NOT SHARE
A TOY WITH
YOUR BROTHER!
GO BACK THREE
SPACES

DID NOT COMPLETE
HOMEWORK!
GO BACK ONE SPACE

FORGOT TO TAKE
OUT THE
GARBAGE!
LOSE A TURN

FORGOT TO FEED
THE FAMILY PETS!
GO BACK TWO
SPACES

TOLD A LIE!
GO BACK THREE
SPACES

CLEANED UP YOUR ROOM!
MOVE AHEAD ONE SPACE

BROUGHT HOME A GOOD STUDENT AWARD!
MOVE AHEAD THREE SPACES

HELPED YOUR MOTHER IN THE KITCHEN!
MOVE AHEAD ONE SPACE

HELPED YOUR YOUNGER BROTHER WITH HIS HOMEWORK!
MOVE AHEAD THREE SPACES

TOOK OUT THE GARBAGE WITHOUT BEING ASKED!
TAKE ANOTHER TURN

SHARED A TOY WITH YOUR SISTER!
MOVE AHEAD TWO SPACES

TURNED IN ALL ASSIGNMENTS AT SCHOOL!
TAKE ANOTHER TURN

BOUGHT A MOTHER'S DAY GIFT FOR YOUR MOM WITH YOUR OWN MONEY!
MOVE AHEAD TWO SPACES

# Mother's Day Coupon Book

This clever coupon book makes a perfect Mother's Day gift.

Copy the coupons onto index paper and have students do the coloring with crayons or colored markers. Punch two holes where indicated and attach the book together with a ribbon or piece of yarn. Children can also add their own coupons using the provided blank pages.

Mother will love receiving this gift and redeeming each coupon!

**Mother's Day Coupon Book**

Redeem this coupon and I'll take out the trash ____ times!

**Mother's Day Coupon Book**

Redeem this coupon and I'll feed our pets ____ times!

Redeem this coupon and I'll help in the kitchen ____ times!

**Mother's Day Coupon Book**

Redeem this coupon and I'll clean my room ____ times!

**Mother's Day Coupon Book**

**Mother's Day Coupon Book**

**Mother's Day Coupon Book**

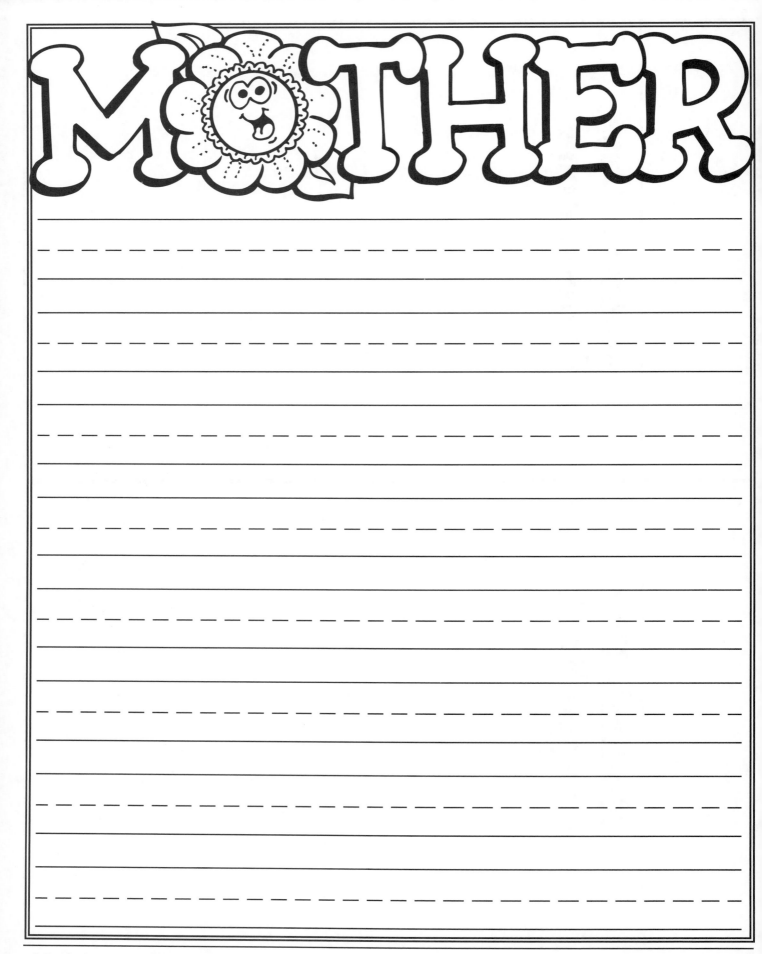

SOCCER ACTIVITIES
SOCCER CHARACTER
SOCCER BOARD GAME
SOCCER BULLETIN BOARDS
CREATIVE WRITING SOCCER BALLS

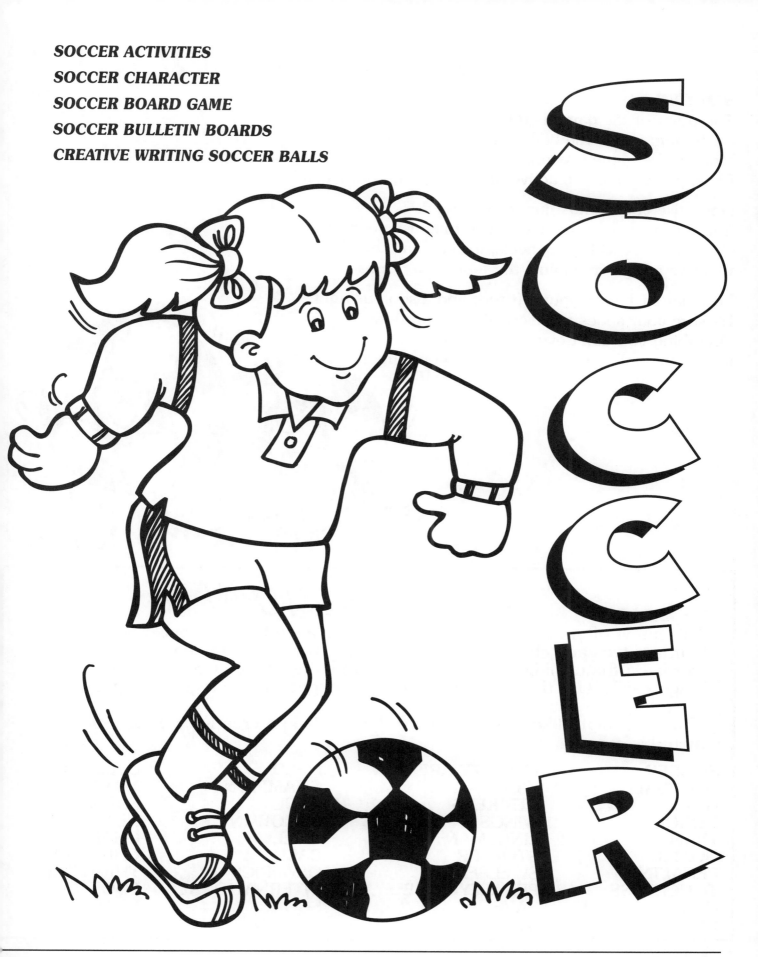

# SOCCER ACTIVITIES!

## SOCCER

The point of the game is the ball to the goal.
Each team wants the ball in its own control.
Most of the game is a run and a kick.
Players' legs must be active and strong and quite quick.

Don't use your hands, just feet instead.
You may use your shoulders; you may use your head.
You may kick with your heels, insteps and toes
to score a big win against the team you oppose.

You may kick with your left foot and also your right.
Be sure your shoes are laced firmly and tight.
One thing you don't ever want to do
is kick the ball and then off comes your shoe!

---

# SOCCER BINGO!

This game offers an exciting way to introduce students to soccer vocabulary words. Give each child a copy of the bingo words listed below or write the words on the chalkboard. Ask students to write any 24 words on his or her bingo cards. Use the same directions you might use for regular bingo.

(Students might like to use some of the words in a creative writing assignment.)

| | | | |
|---|---|---|---|
| SOCCER | PENALTY AREA | FIELD | DEFENDER |
| FOOTBALL | KICK | CHAMPION | MIDFIELDER |
| GOAL | STRIKERS | FOUL | FORWARD |
| PERIOD | WINGS | THROW-IN | NET |
| TEAM | LINKSMAN | WALL | CHARGING |
| GOALIE | STOPPER | BALL | CHEST TAP |
| PENALTY | SWEEPER | OLYMPICS | THIGH TAP |
| TOUCHLESS | PENALTY ZONE | INTERNATIONAL | FOOT TAP |
| CENTER CIRCLE | SAVE | SCORE | HEAD TAP |
| GOAL AREA | REFEREE | POINTS | PLAYER |

---

# KICK FOR

**TEACHERS:** Make your own task cards for this game that two, three or four children can play.

TF1603 Spring Idea Book

# THE GOAL!

# Soccer Character!

Make this cute character from index paper. Color, cut out and fold. Bend his arms forward and staple or paste the ball to his hands.

# Creative Writing Soccer Balls!

Everyone laughed when a player from both teams received a penalty for...

The score was tied when, in the last few seconds, the impossible happened!

He kicked the ball so high that it went clear out of sight!

TF1603 Spring Idea Book

The referee suddenly stopped the game when...

The team's new mascot made the crowd roar with laughter!

The crowd went wild as the goalie dove for the ball!

TF1603 Spring Idea Book

# SOCCER BULLETIN BOARDS!

## GOALS FOR THE FUTURE!

Motivate your students to examine their future goals with this easy bulletin board. Enlarge these cute soccer characters with an overhead projector and display them on the board. Children can write poems or creative stories about their goals for the next school year or occupations they may wish to have when they are grown.

## KICK-OFF FACTS!

Children can review their multiplication tables with this simple bulletin board. Display a large soccer ball made from black and white construction paper. Write multiplication problems on each section of the ball. As a class, review the answers after the students have worked the problems at their desks.

---

TF1603 Spring Idea Book

# SOCCER BALL